To Christopher from
Mommy & Daddy
Oct 25, 1982

On your 1st baptismal
anniversary

Prayers
for the Very Young
Child

PRAYERS
FOR THE VERY YOUNG CHILD

Written by
Donald S. Roberts
Illustrated by
Patricia Mattozzi

**With thanks to God
with whose help they were written,
I dedicate these prayers
to my son Sean,
and to children everywhere.**

Copyright © 1981 by Concordia Publishing House
3558 South Jefferson Avenue, St. Louis, MO 63118

Printed in the United States of America

Library of Congress Cataloging in Publication Data

Roberts, Donald S 1946-
    Prayers for the very young child.

    SUMMARY: Contains 60 prayers in 3 categories: daily,
table, and bedtime prayers.
    1. Children—Prayer-books and devotions—English.
[1. Prayers] I. Title.
BV4870.R6 242'.82   80-22229
ISBN 0-570-04051-5

---

1 2 3 4 5 6 7 8 9 10 DB 90 89 88 87 86 85 84 83 82 81

Table of Contents

DAILY PRAYERS

Let me make You happy, Lord,
With every action, every word.
Never let me drift away,
Make me Yours, dear Lord, each day.

Thank You for the gifts, Lord,
That come from You each day.
Thank You for my parents' love.
Watch over them I pray.

I am Your child, oh dearest Lord.
Each day I pray to Thee.
Help me to love all people
The way that You love me.

Lord, this prayer is not for me.
It's for my little friends.
Watch over each of them, I pray,
As each new day begins.

Forgive me, Lord, if I have done
Some things to make You sad.
Show me now the way to do
The things that make You glad.

Bless me, dearest Lord, I pray
That I may bless someone today.
Show me how to share Your joy
With every girl and every boy.

Thank You for the world so bright.
Thank You for the warm sunlight.
Thank You for the stars above.
Thank You for Your endless love.

Dearest Jesus, lead the way
Through the coming hours of day.
Keep me safe in all I do
Ever close, my Lord, to You.

Thank You, God, that we are one.
Thank You for your loving Son.
Thank You that to make me free,
Jesus came to die for me.

Teach me to be thankful, Lord,
In everything I do.
For all the things I call my own
Are really gifts from You.

Jesus, hear me as I pray.
Keep all people safe today.
Watch them from Your home above.
Send each one Your Father's love.

Lord, teach me to be kind,
To never hurt another.
Lord, let me see all people
As my sisters and my brothers.

In everyone I meet, oh Lord,
Let me find the good.
Help me to love each one, dear Lord,
The way I know You would.

Thank You for my mother,
And for my father too.
They are loving, kind, and true,
My greatest gifts from You.

Father, keep me close to You.
Show me the things that I should do.
In Your care, Lord, all the while
Teach me how to be Your child.

Thank You for the rainbow,
And for the gentle rain
That makes the trees and flowers grow.
Thank You, God, again.

When I am sick, dear Jesus,
Come take away my pain.
Touch me with Your healing hands,
And make me well again.

Dearest Father, come to me.
Live inside my heart.
Keep me ever close to You.
Never let us part.

Thank You for the fluffy clouds
That float up in the sky.
Thank You for this world so good
That shines inside my eyes.

Thank You, Lord, for all my toys.
I use them every day.
Thank You that I am healthy, Lord,
So I can run and play.

Thank You, Lord, for Sunday School,
And for my teacher dear.
Who tells me all about You,
And makes You seem so near.

I love You, dearest Jesus,
And I know that You love me.
Help everyone to know, dear Lord,
That's just as it should be.

TABLE
PRAYERS

**Bless this food
Dear Lord, we pray.
Make us thankful every day.**

Bless the one who cooks this food
And places it here before me.
For all the love that here is shown,
Dearest Lord, I thank Thee.

Lord, be present at our table.
We thank You that we now are able
To welcome friends our food to share
By Your grace and loving care.

Father, on this special day
Thanks for all Your love, we pray.
For this meal our thanks we give.
Help us in Your grace to live.

Thank You, Lord, that in Your care
You are with us everywhere.
Bless our food and us in Thee,
Wherever we may choose to be.

Now we bow our head to pray.
Thank You for this food today.
Now we fold our hands and say,
Thank You, Lord, in every way.

Come, oh Jesus, to our table.
For Your sweet love alone is able
To make us thankful for this food,
And all God's gifts so great and good.

Surrounded, Lord, by flowers and trees,
Beneath Your sky of blue,
We thank You now on bended knee
For this food which comes from You.

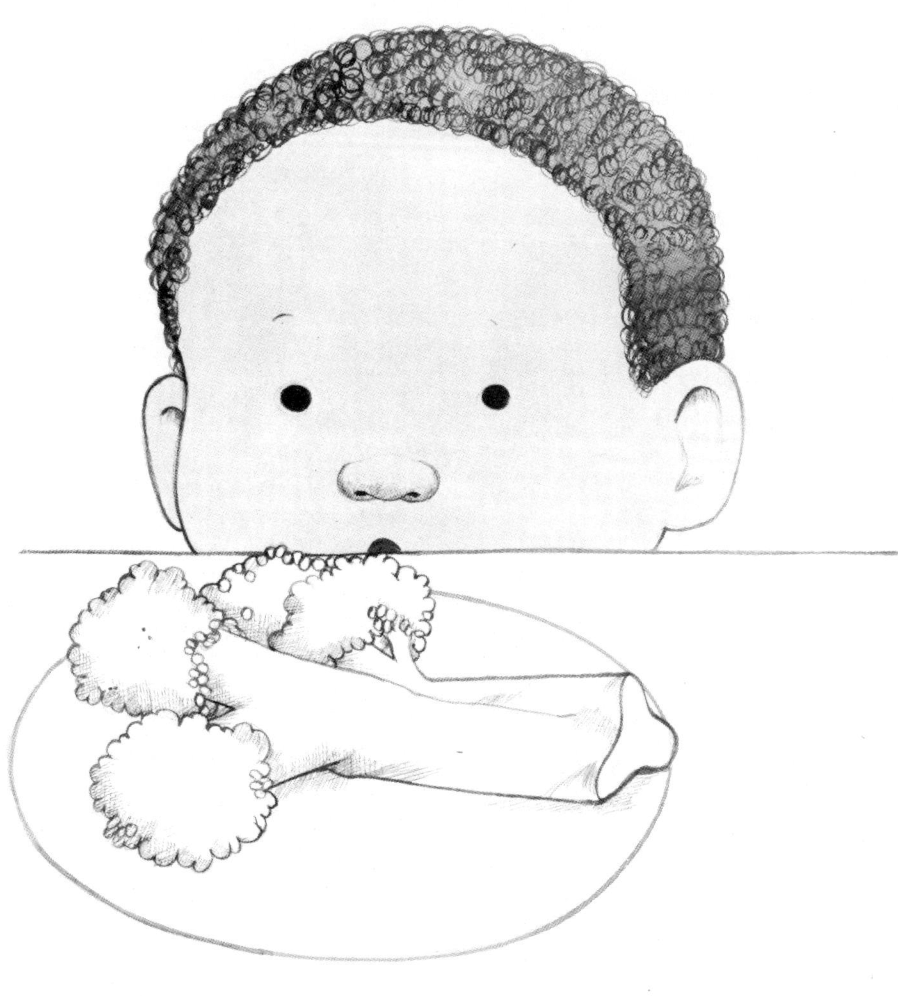

**Father, make me thankful
For food that may not be
The food I think it's best to eat,
But still is good for me.**

Thanks, oh dearest Lord, we pray,
For the food You give each day.
Keep us thankful for our place
At Your table full of grace.

Come, oh Father,
Loving and good.
Bless Your child,
And bless this food.

Thank You for this special meal.
Dear Father, help me see,
That every gift and blessing,
Shows all Your love for me.

I do not have to speak, my Lord,
For You to know my every word.
Now in silence hear me pray,
Bless to me this food today.

**Thank You as we gather here
That You have given grandparents dear
To share this meal with us today
For their love our thanks we pray.**

Make us thankful for this food.
Bless us, Father, as You would.
Keep us near to You this day.
Hear us, Father, as we pray.

Thank You, Lord, that I may be
Here with all my family.
Thank You for each blessing good.
Thank You for this gift of food.

As we gather here with friends
Let Your love, Lord, enter in.
Make us thankful as we share
This meal, this friendship, and this prayer.

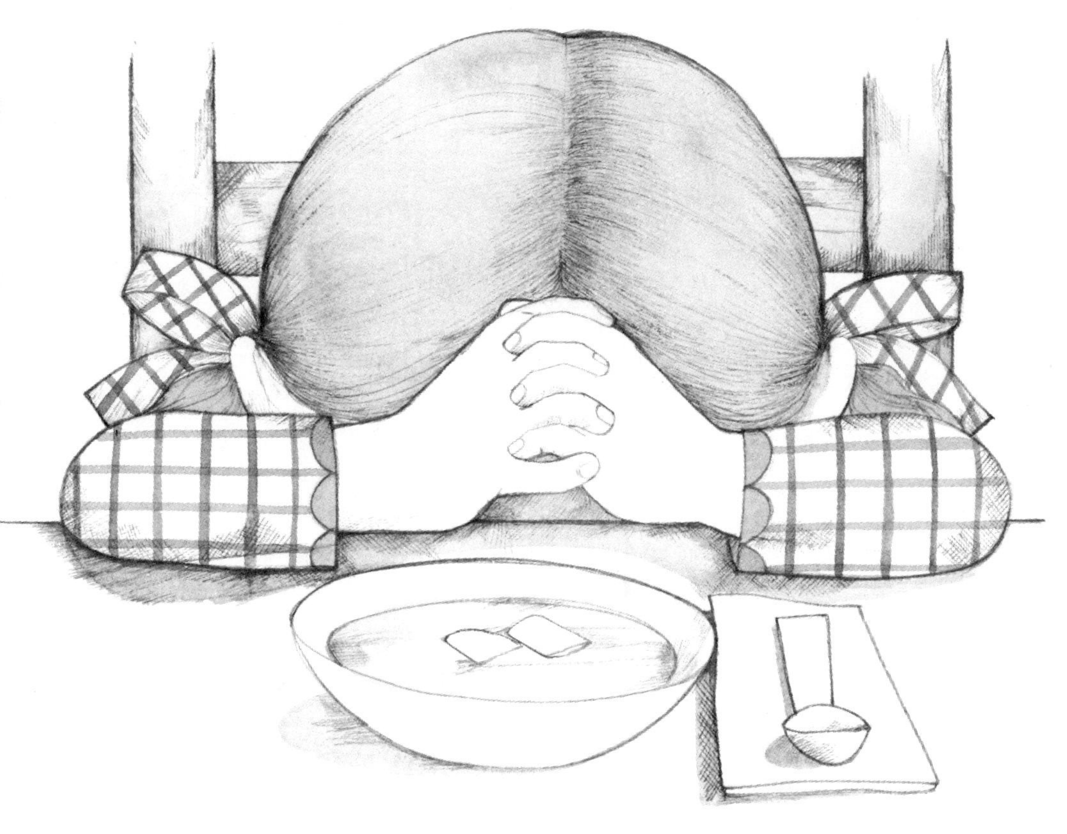

Thank You for this meal, dear Lord,
Thank You for Your living Word.
As I pray with head bowed low,
In Your service let me grow.

Heavenly Father, let me see,
All the ways that You bless me.
Thank You for the food I'm fed,
Thank You for my daily bread.

Father, take a hungry child,
Hold him to Your breast awhile.
Feed him, Father, let him be,
Blessed the way that You bless me.

BEDTIME PRAYERS

Dearest Lord, before I sleep,
I kneel in prayer to say
Thank You for the world so good,
And for Your love each day.

Dearest Lord, I come to Thee.
Please hear me as I pray.
Keep me safe all through the night,
And bring a bright new day.

Gentle Jesus, hear my prayer.
Keep me safe this night.
Stay with me until the dark
Becomes the morning light.

Dearest Jesus, come to me.
Keep Your watch of love.
Keep me in Your love I pray,
Tonight and through the coming day.

Before I close my eyes so tight,
I pray Thee watch me through the night.
Stay beside me, Lord, to keep
Me safe while in my dreams I sleep.
And when the night has passed away,
Bring to me a brand new day.

For keeping me all through the day,
For watching while I was at play,
I thank You, Lord, and pray You'll keep
Me safe and snug while I'm asleep.

As my eyes You touch with sleep
Your little child I pray Thee keep.
Until the light comes peeping in,
And it is time to play again.

Now another day is through,
Precious Lord, I come to You.
To thank You for each loving gift
As off to sleep I gently drift.
Keep me safe 'til morning comes
Shining with the friendly sun.

Heavenly Father, thanks I pray
For all that You have done this day.
Now keep me safe from every harm,
And let me sleep in Your sweet arms.

Now it's time to go to bed.
I kneel to pray and bow my head.
I thank You, God, for keeping me
Safe and ever near to Thee.
And if in slumber I should stay,
Take me home to heaven I pray.

Hold me in Your hands, oh Lord,
And as I pray hear every word.
Keep me in Your care this night,
And wake me with the morning light.

Now as I close my eyes in prayer
Come to me, sweet Lord, so fair.
Hear the loving words I say.
Keep me safe tonight I pray.
And when tomorrow shines so new
Keep me ever close to You.

Once again its time to pray.
I've had another busy day.
But now it's time to go to sleep.
Dear Jesus, watch me now and keep
Me safe to wake, to run and play
As I receive the coming day.

Now it is the end of day.
The stars so bright come out to play.
Now the time has come to pray.
Now I bow my head and say,
"I love You, dearest Jesus.
Please keep me safe, sweet Jesus."

My Lord, each night I come to You,
When the light of day is through
To give You thanks for all the love
You send to me from heaven.
May everything I say and do
Shine with the love that comes from You.

Lord Jesus, keep me in Thy sight
Through the coming hours of night.
Then when morning sunlight beams
Wake me, Lord, from sleepy dreams.

Dearest Jesus, be my light,
Through the darkest hours of night.
Watch and keep Your little one,
Until You bring the morning sun.

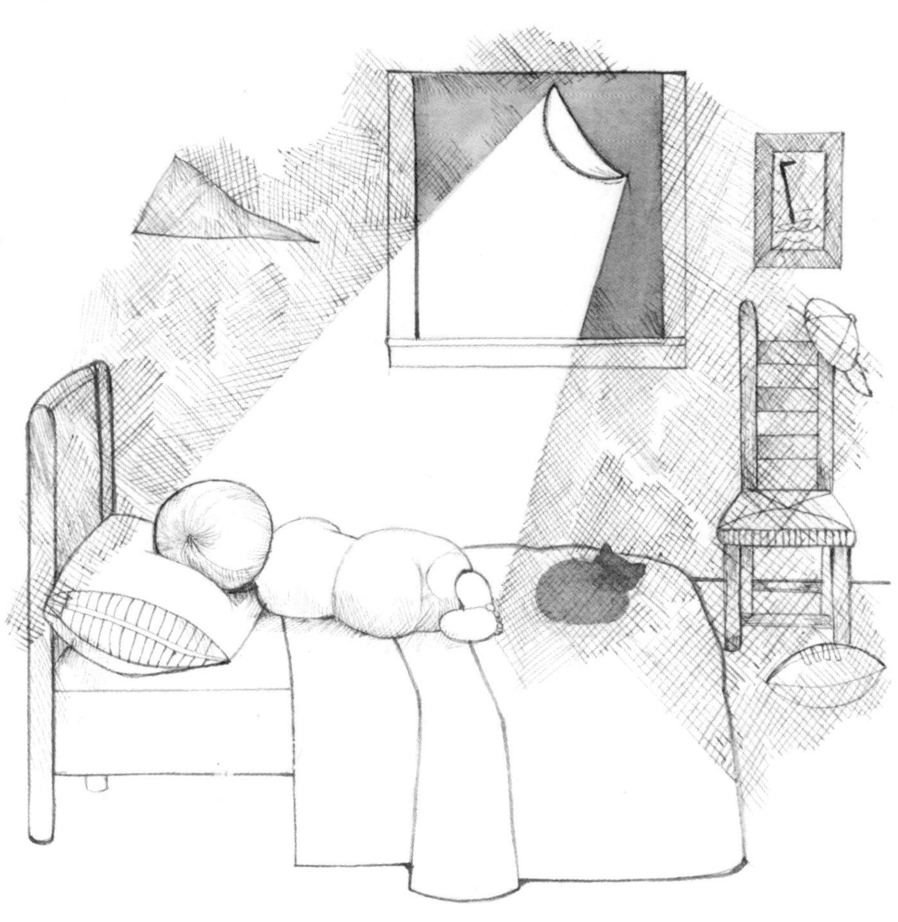

Father now I pray to Thee
Through the night stay close to me.
Bless me now with quiet sleep
As Your loving watch You keep.